WELCOME
TO
COLOR ME BOTANICALS IV
- AN ADULT COLORING BOOK -

ISBN: 1522938710
ISBN-13: 978-1522938712

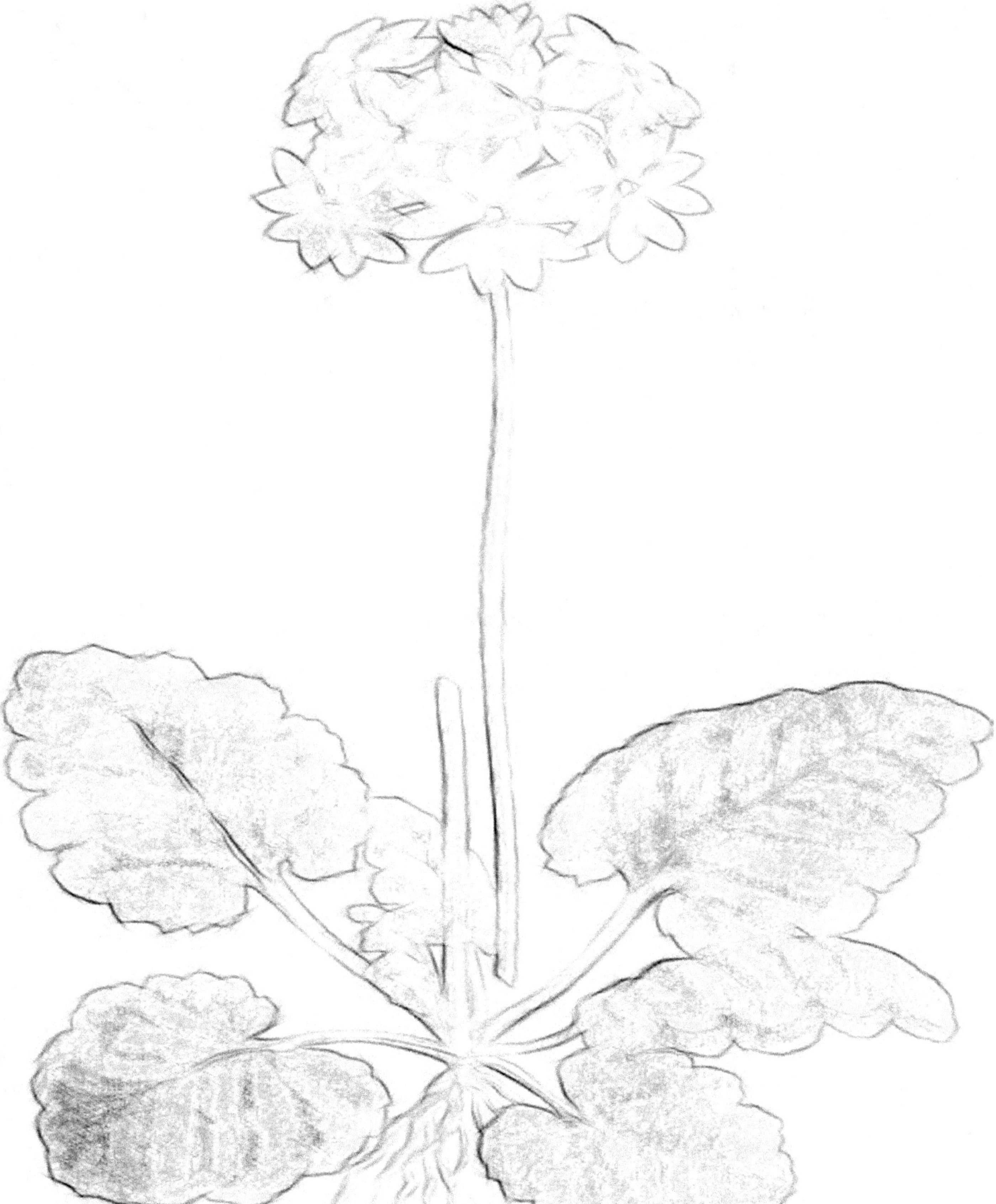

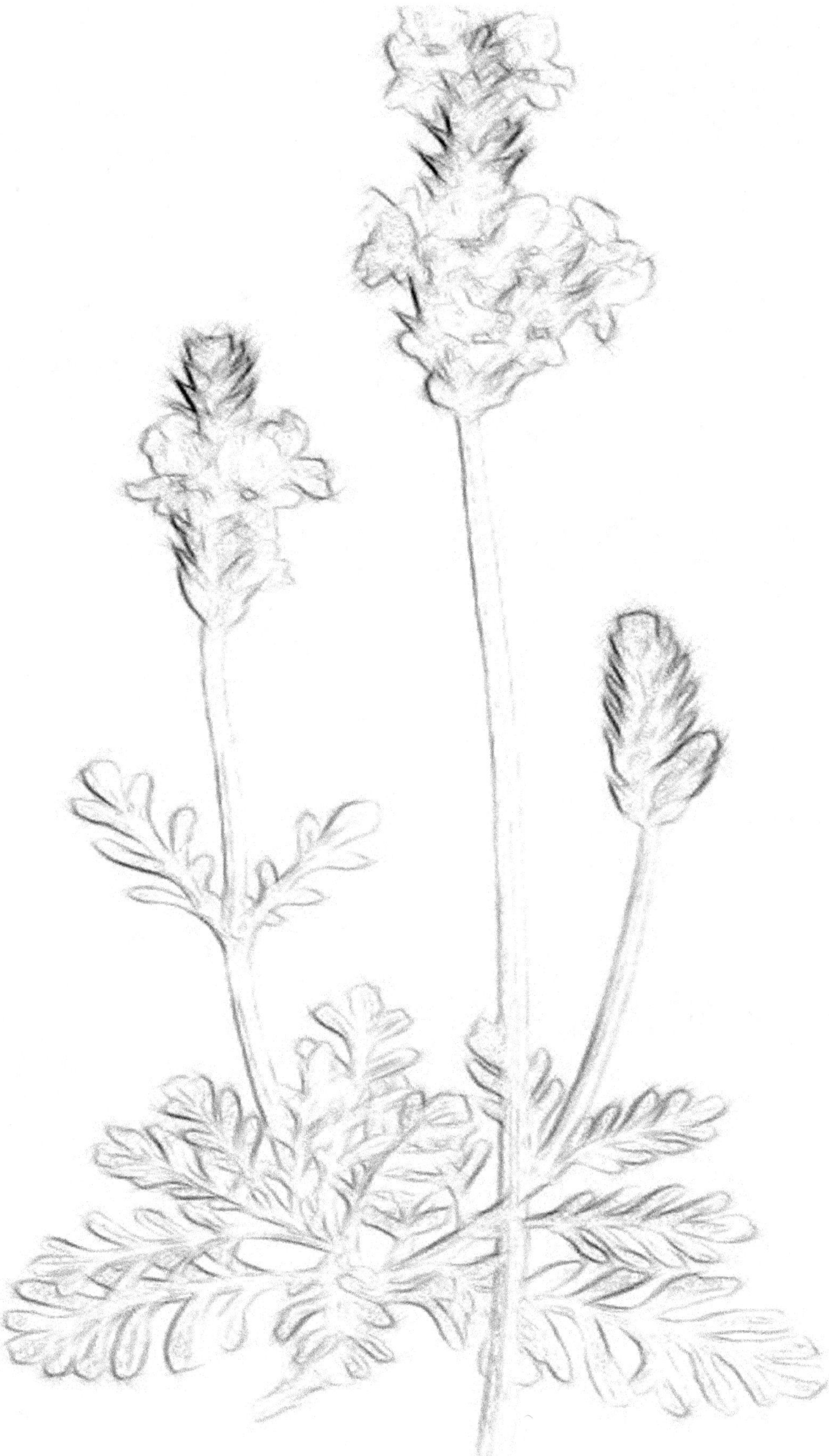

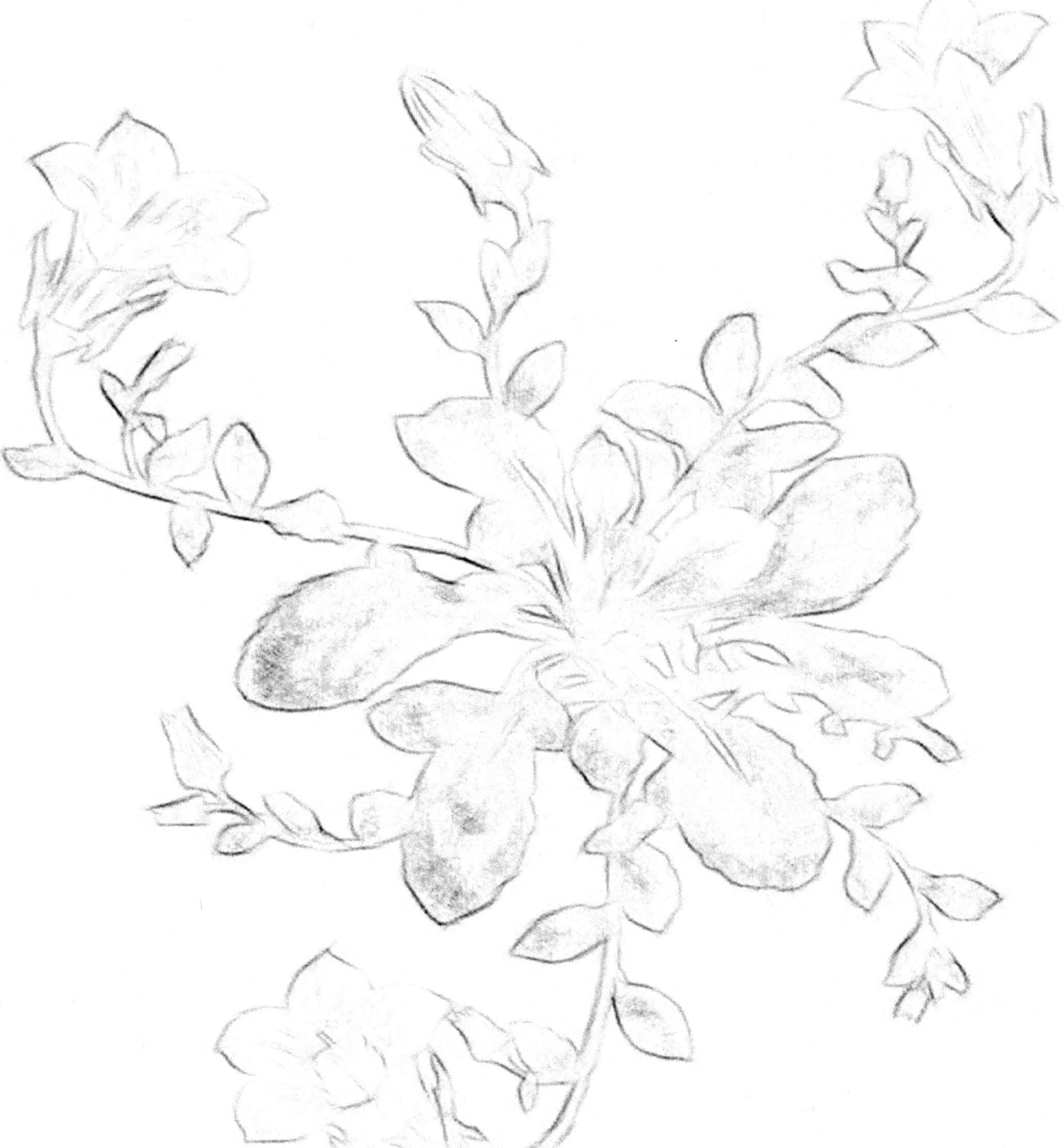

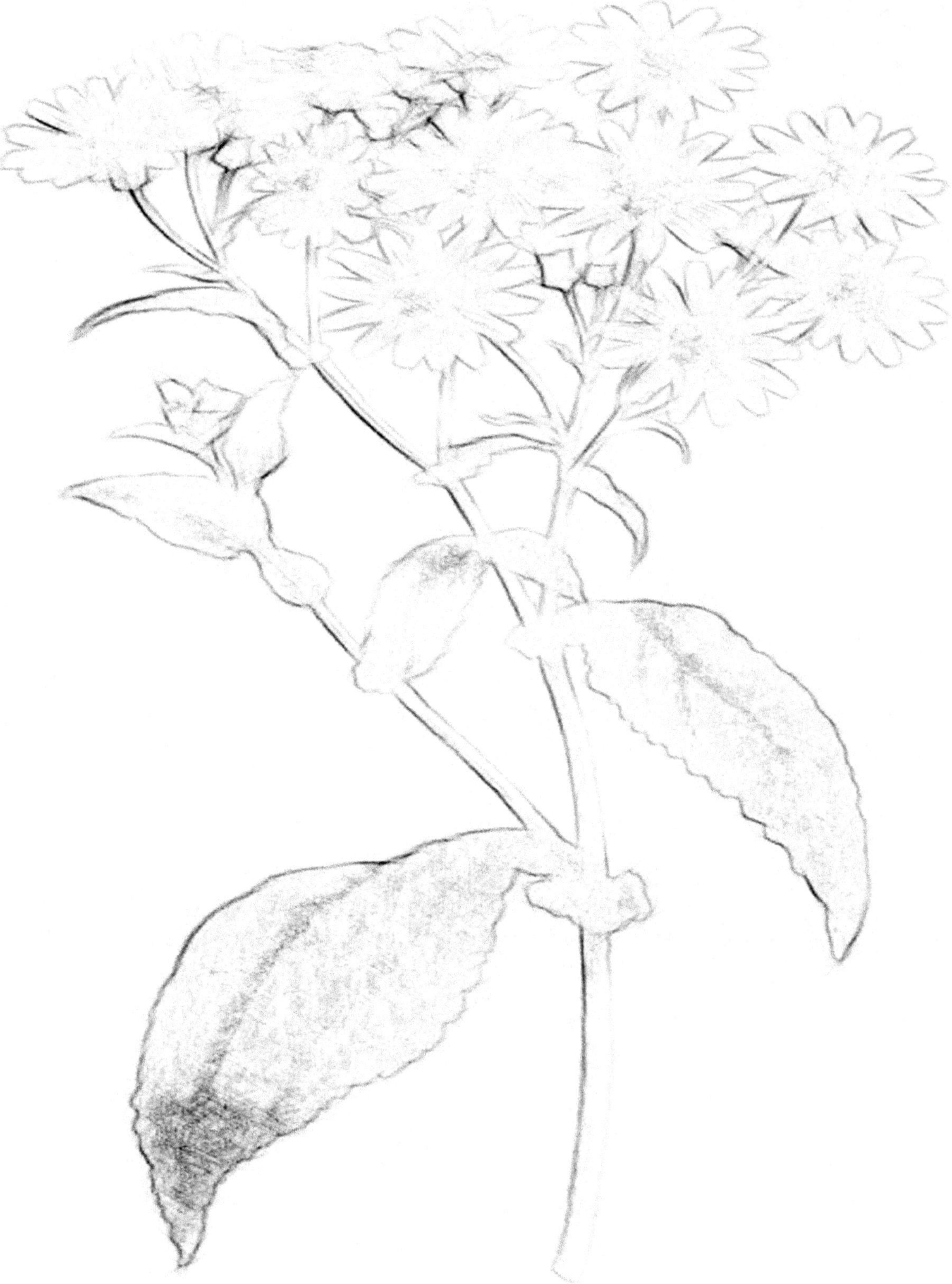

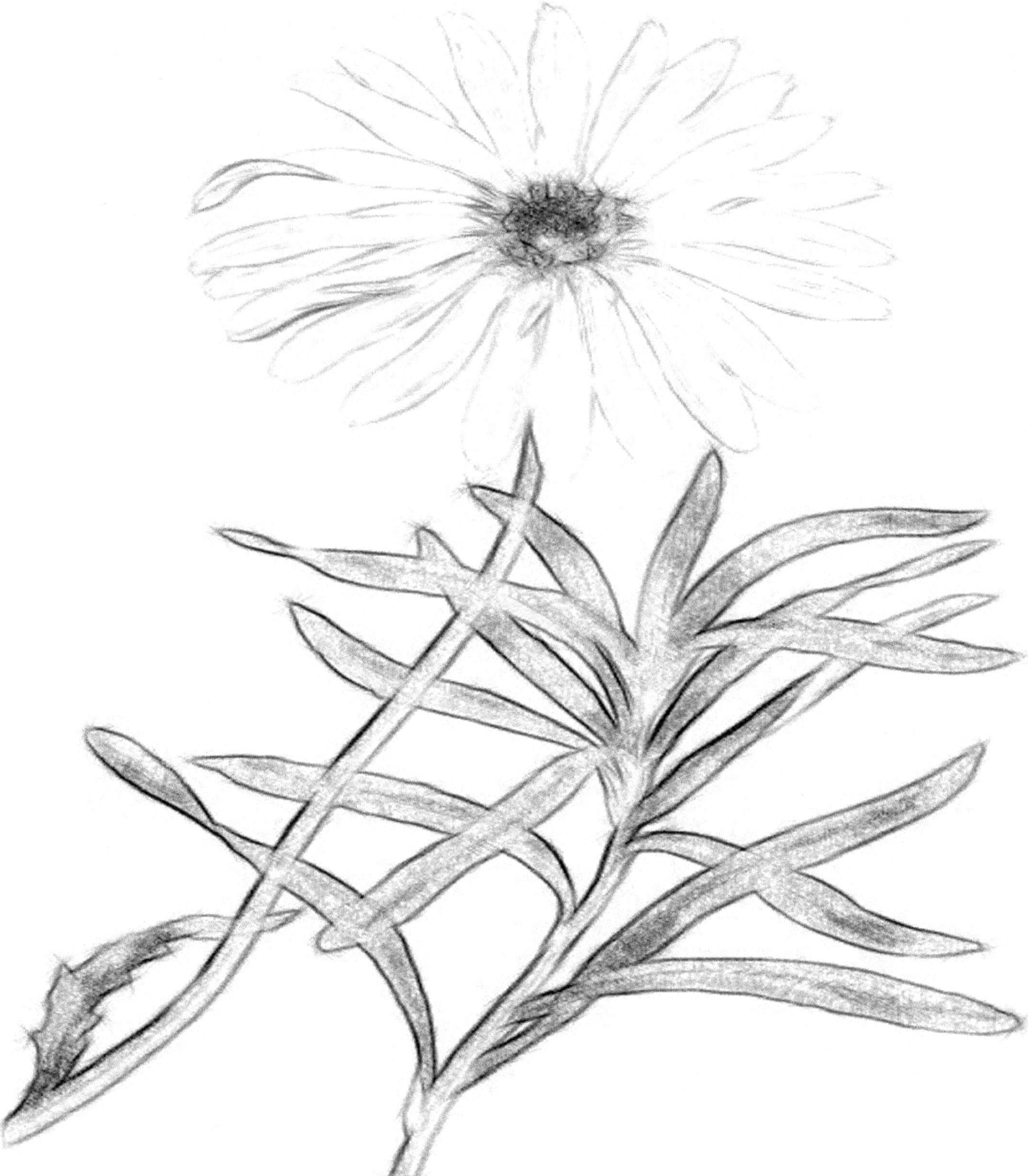

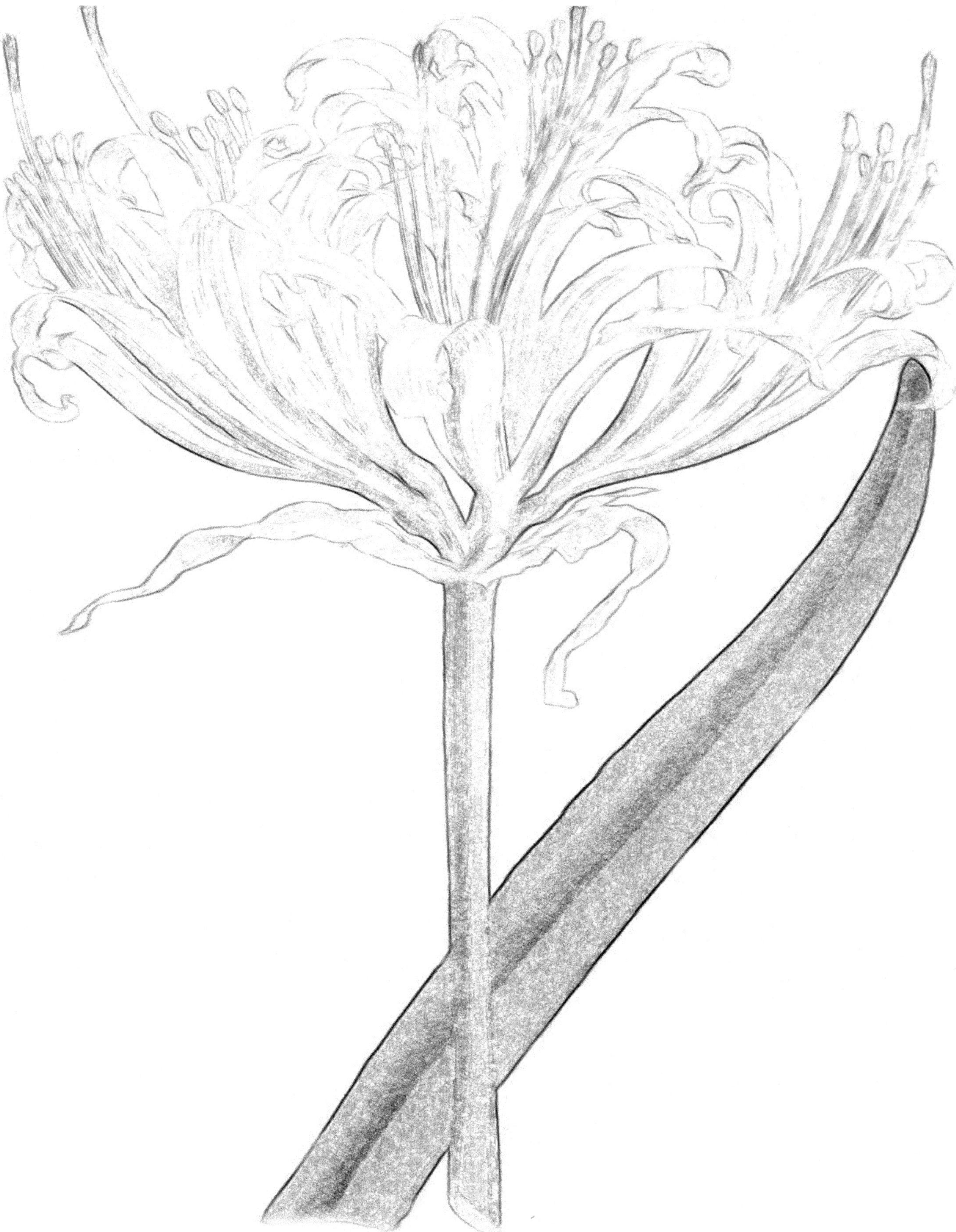

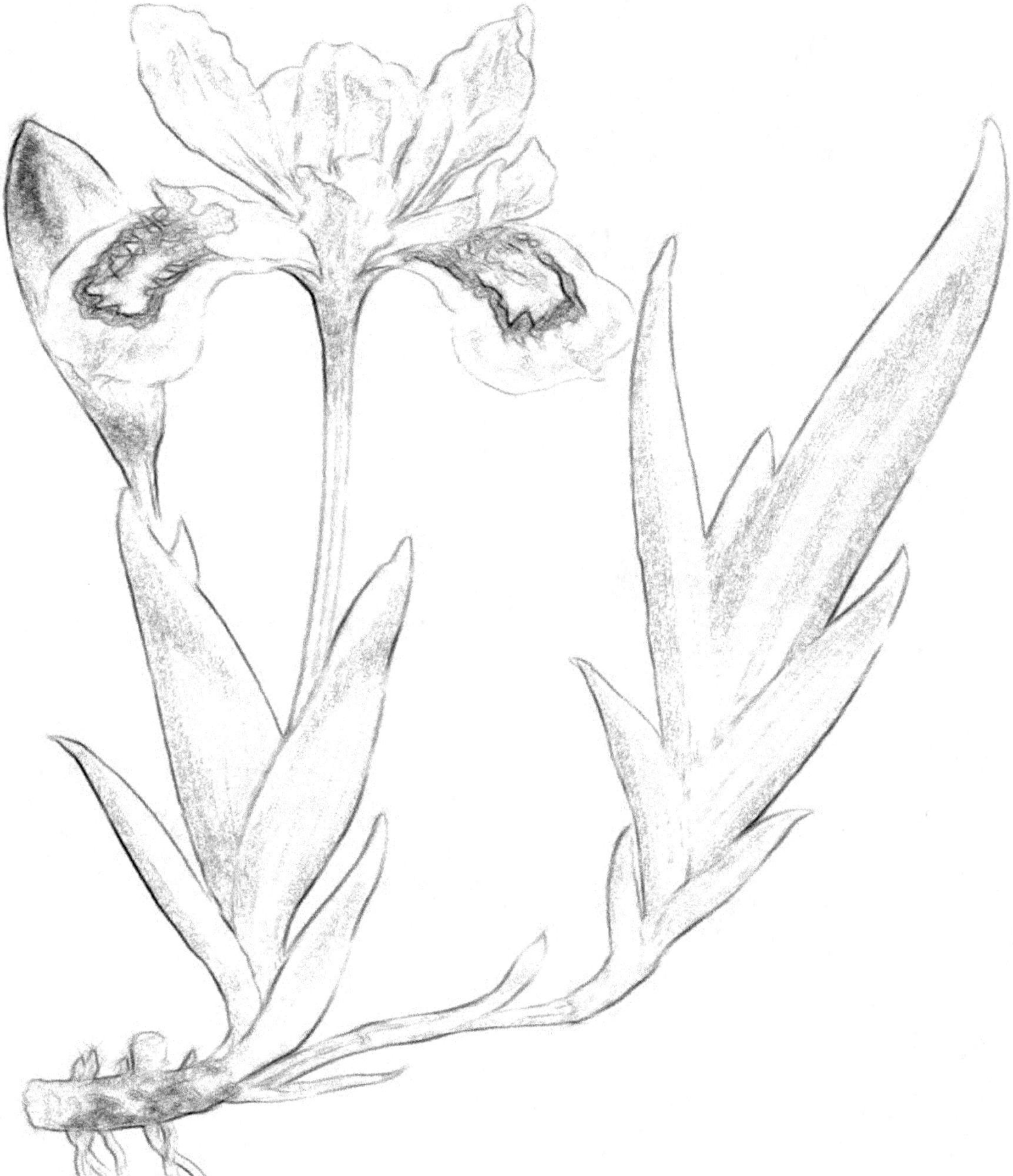

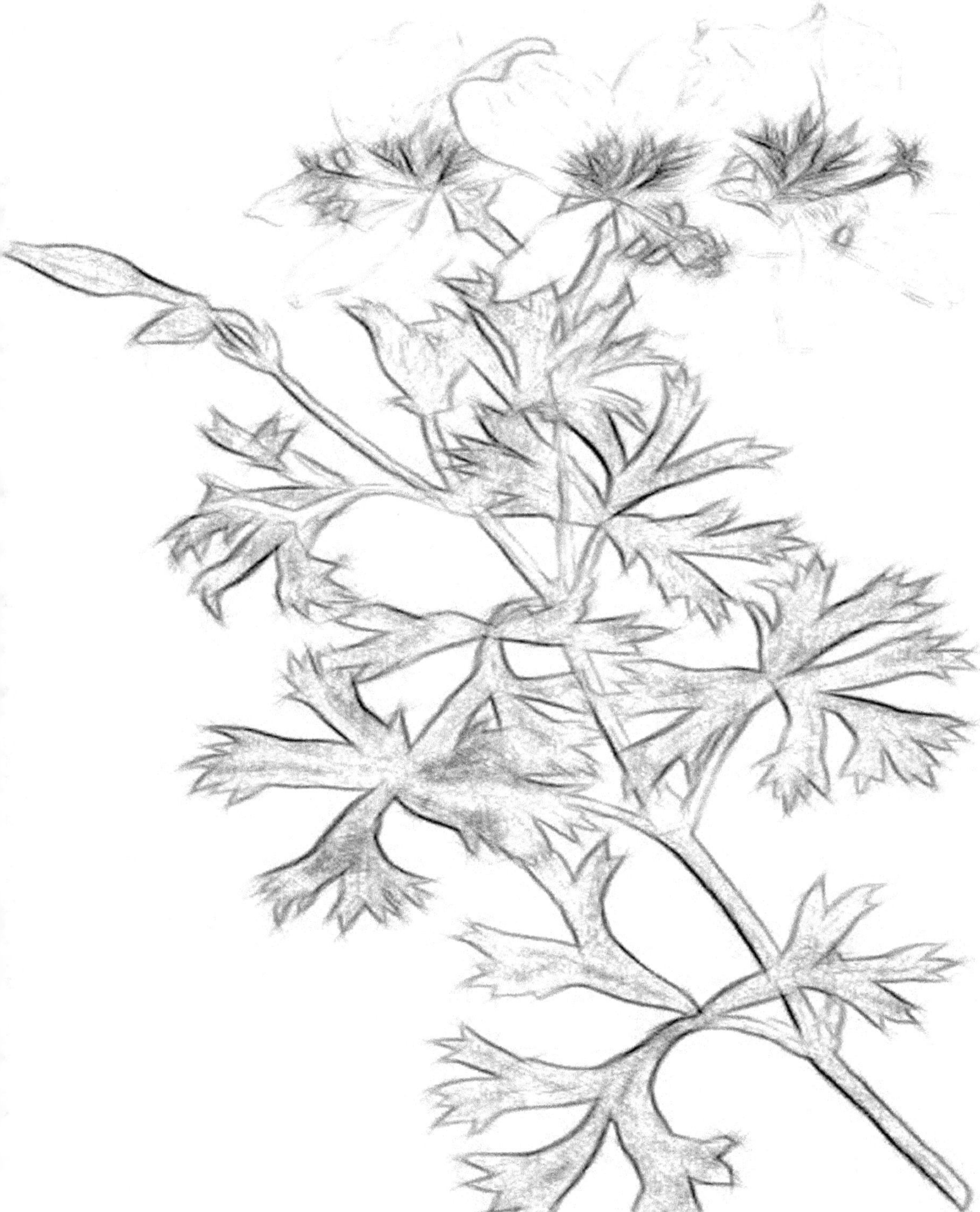

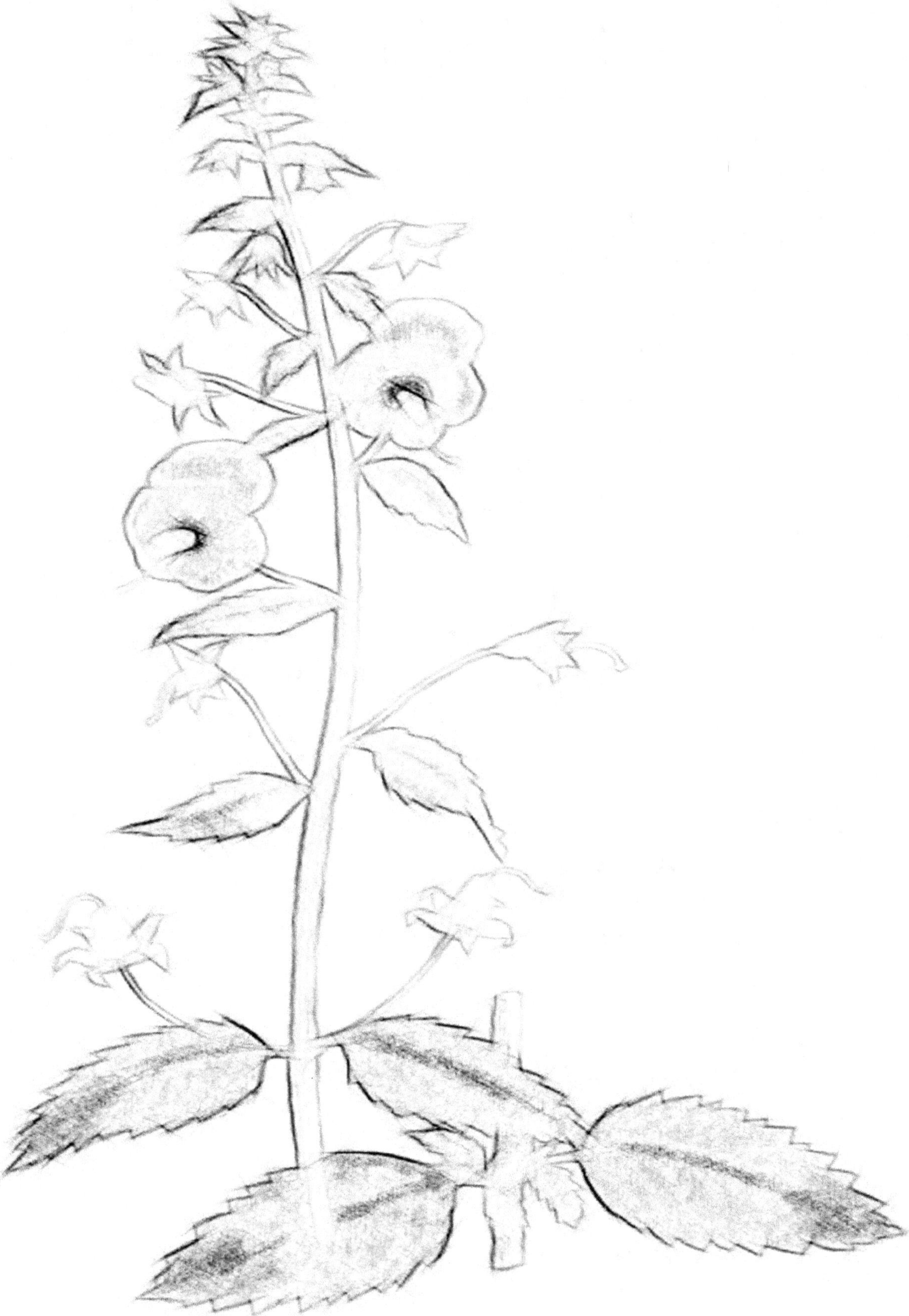

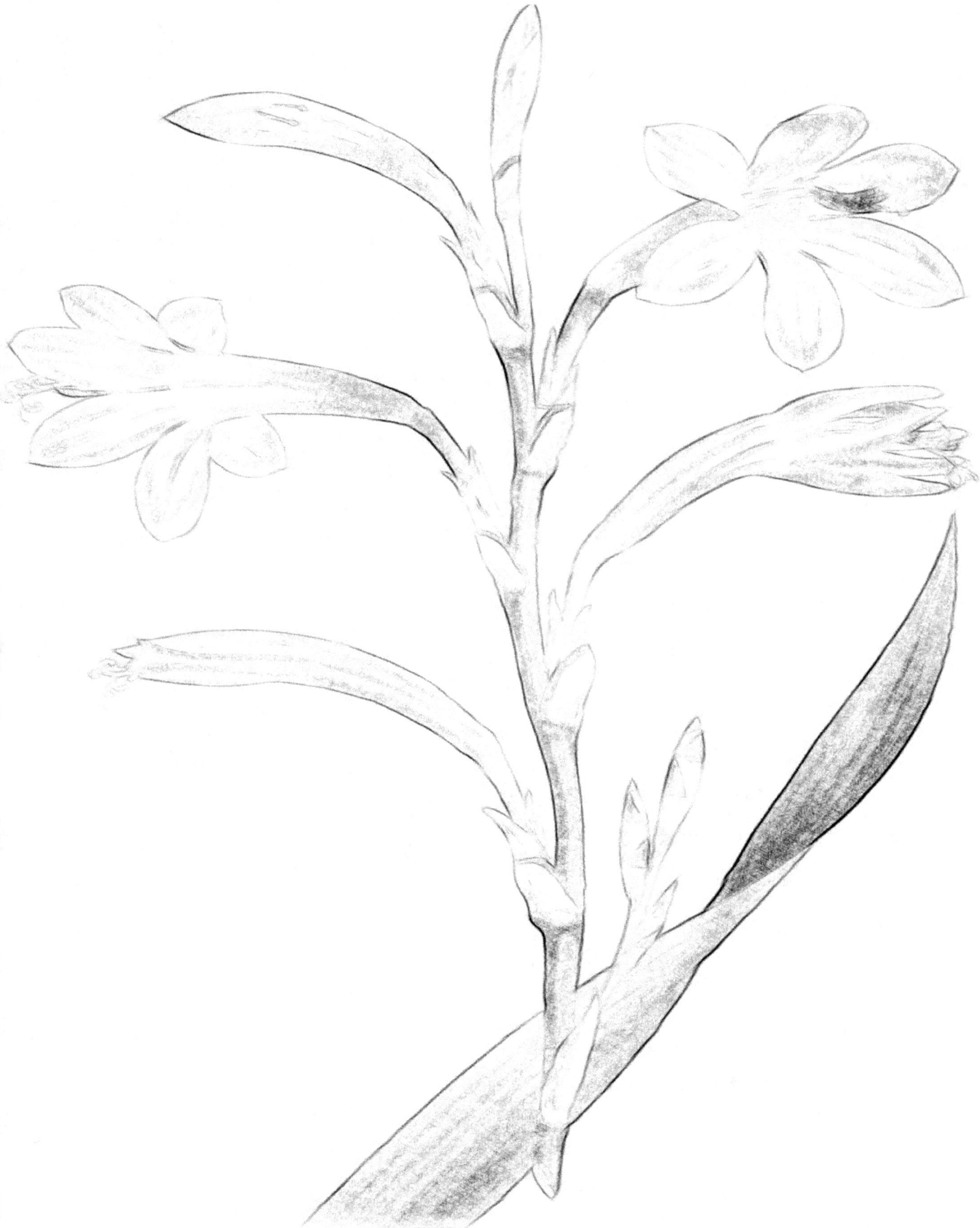

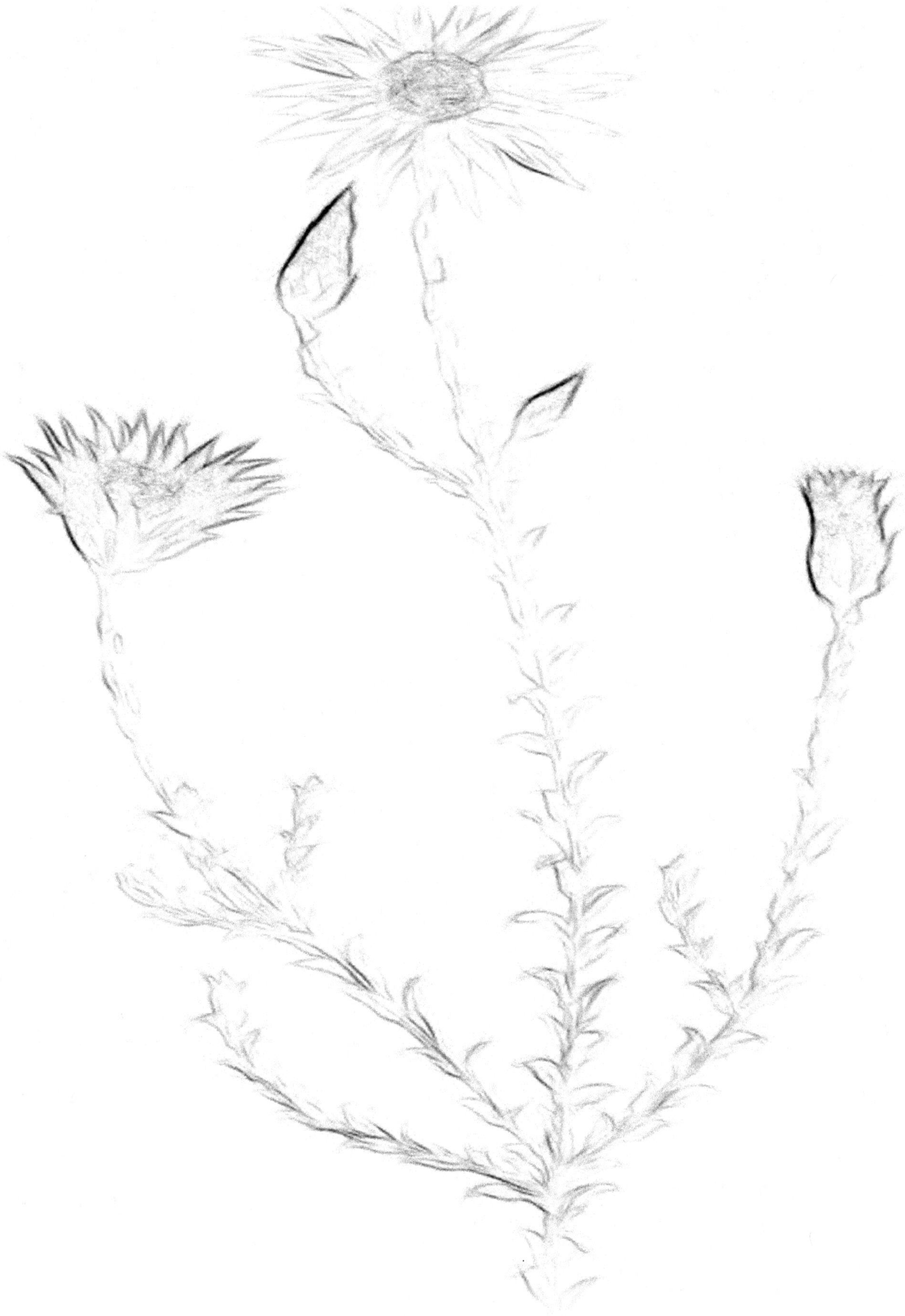

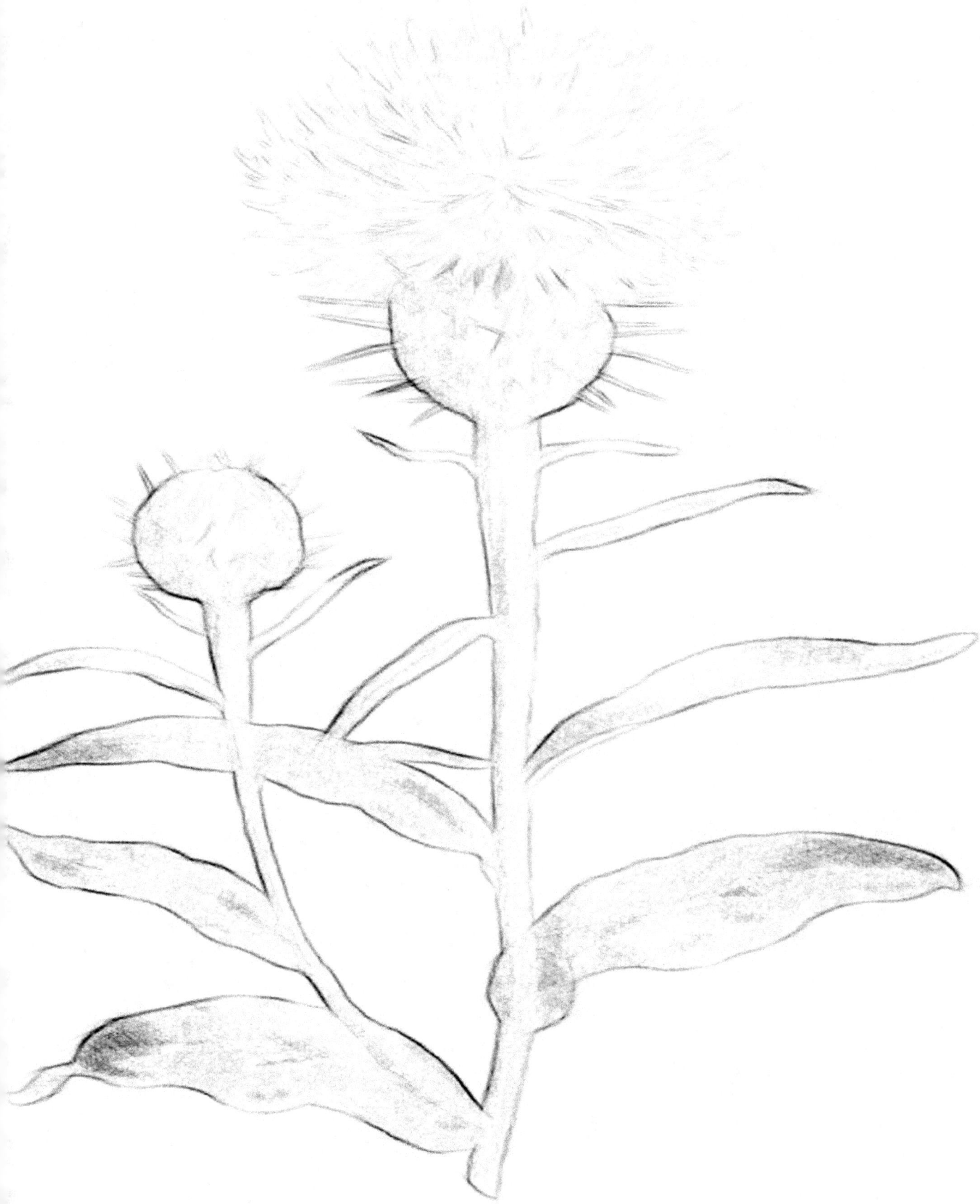

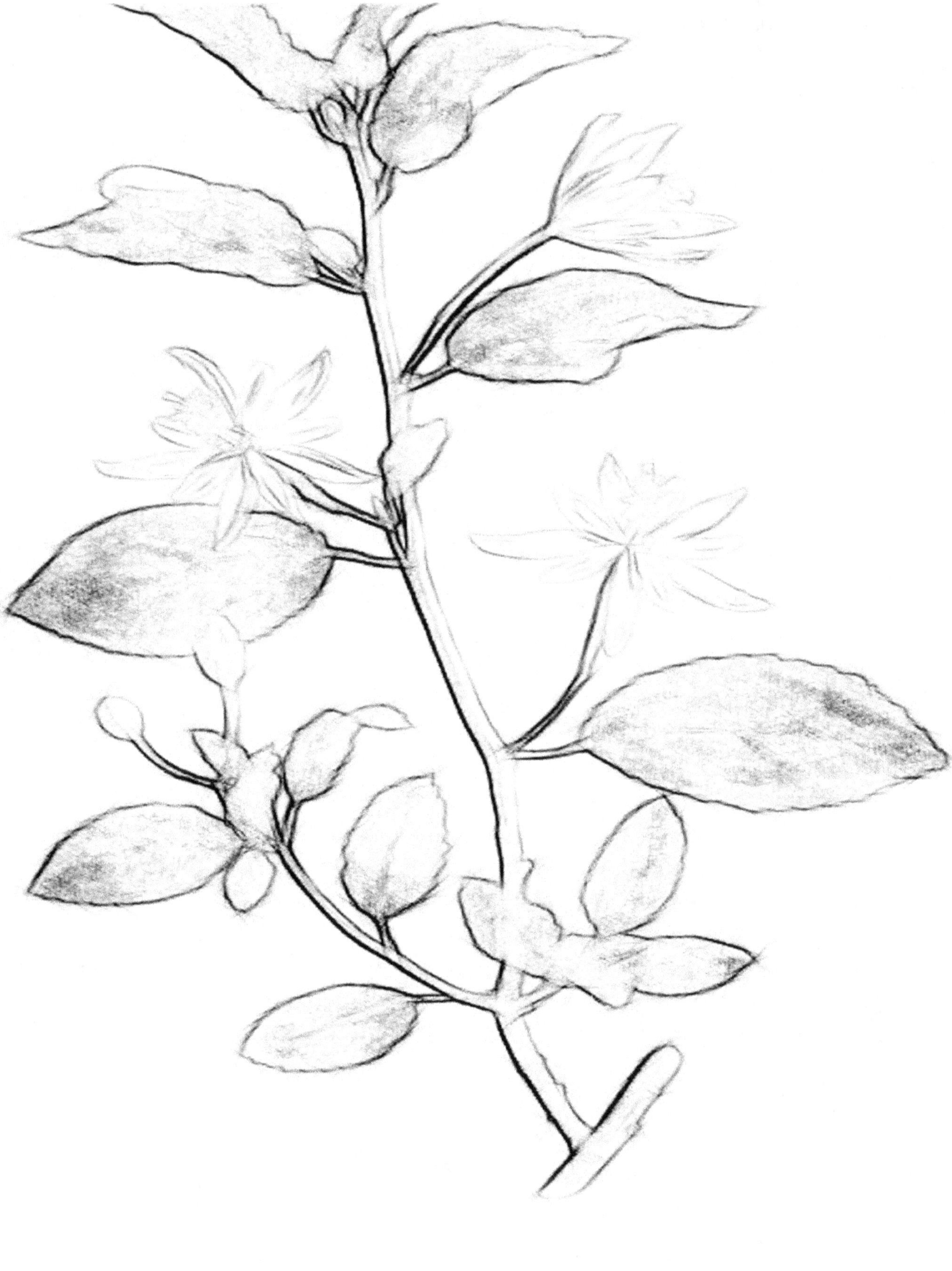

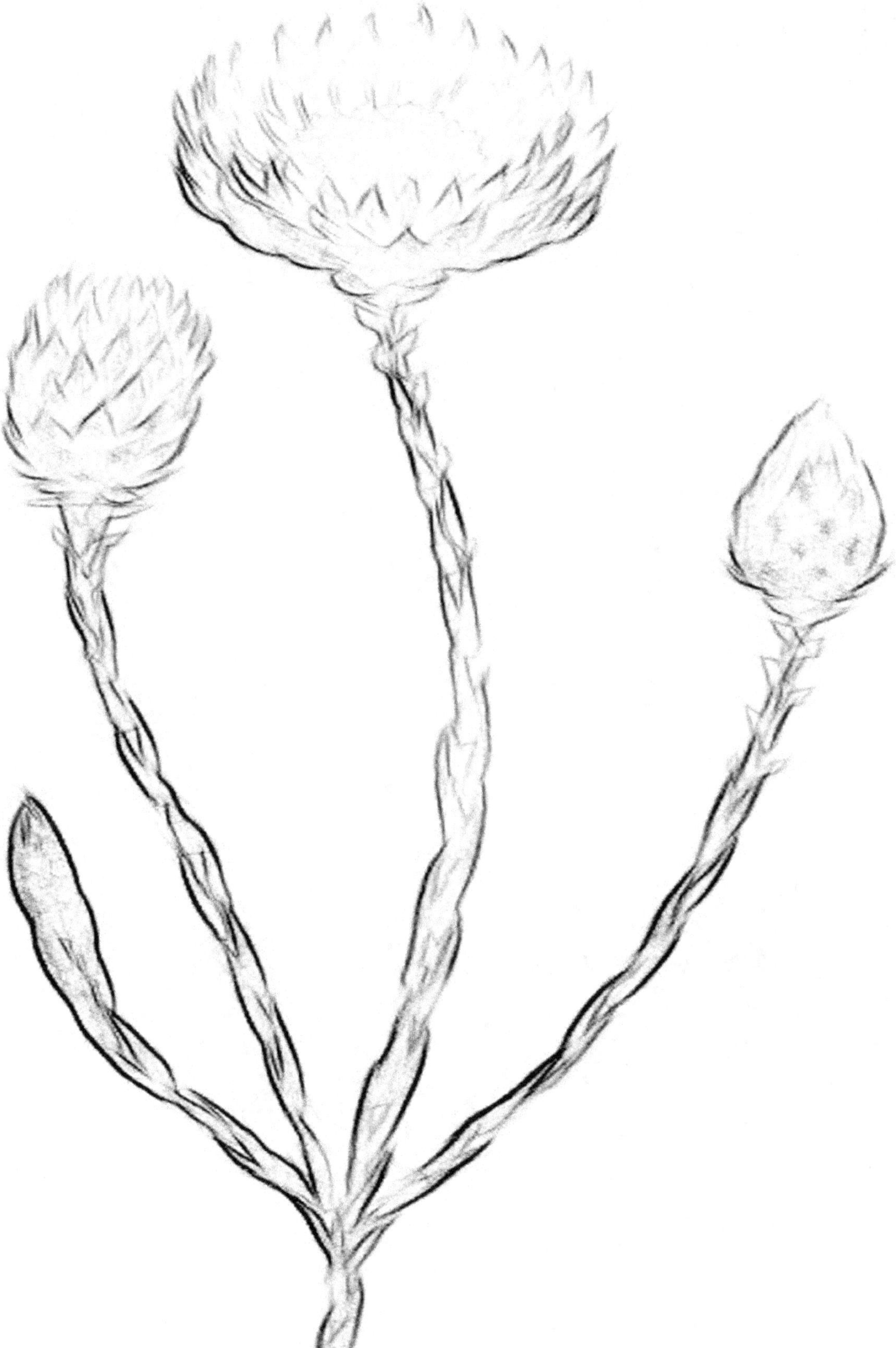

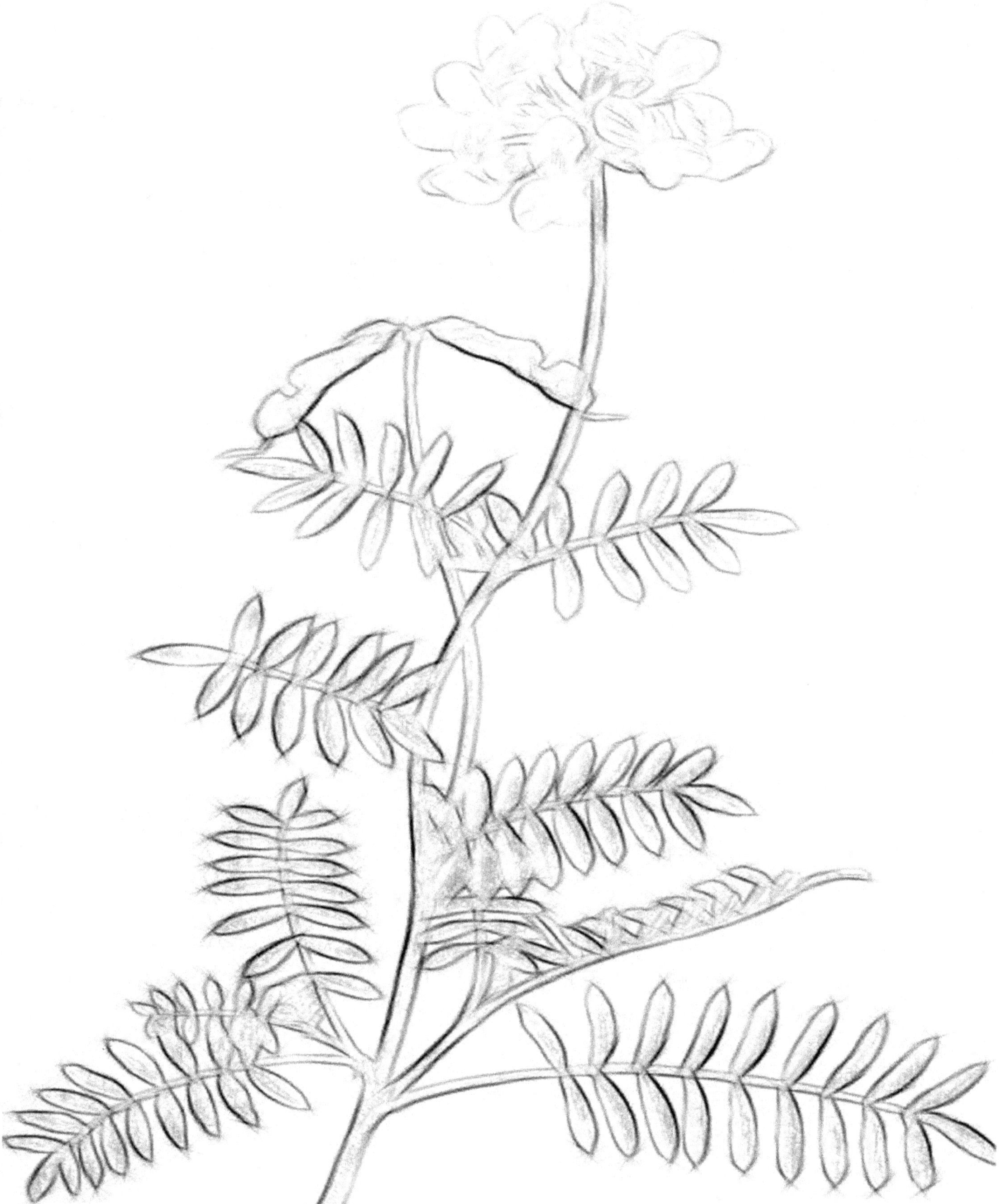

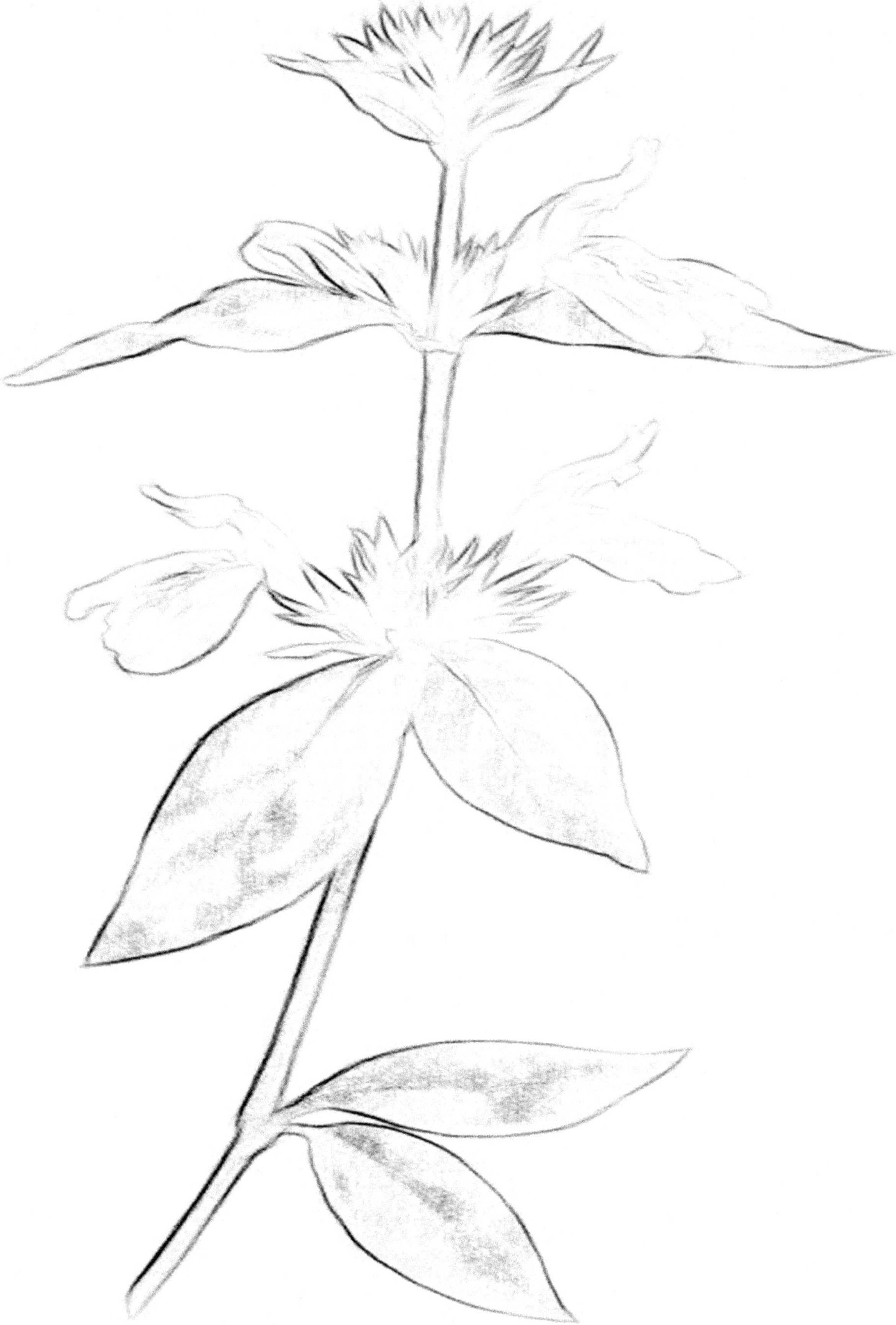

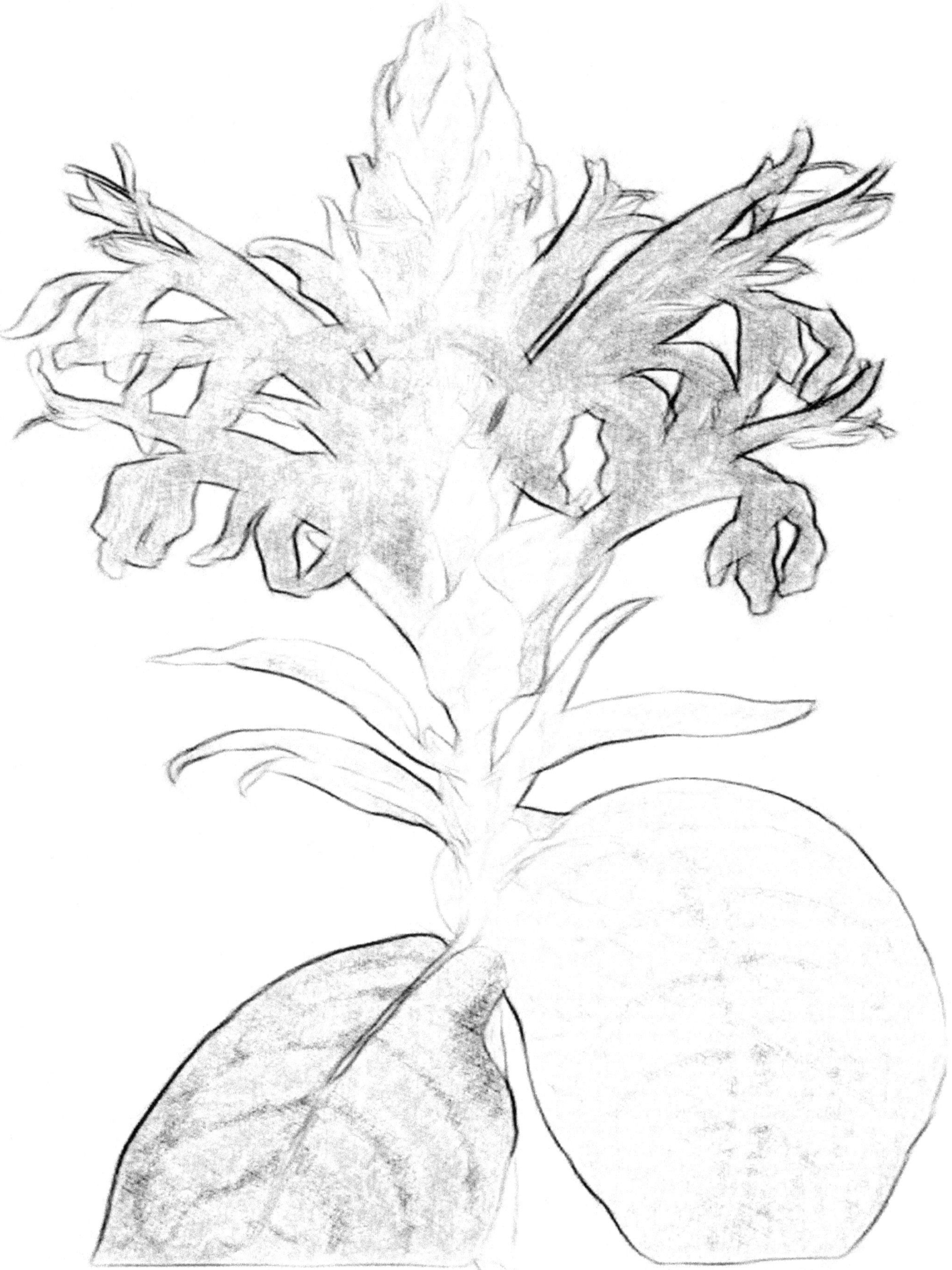

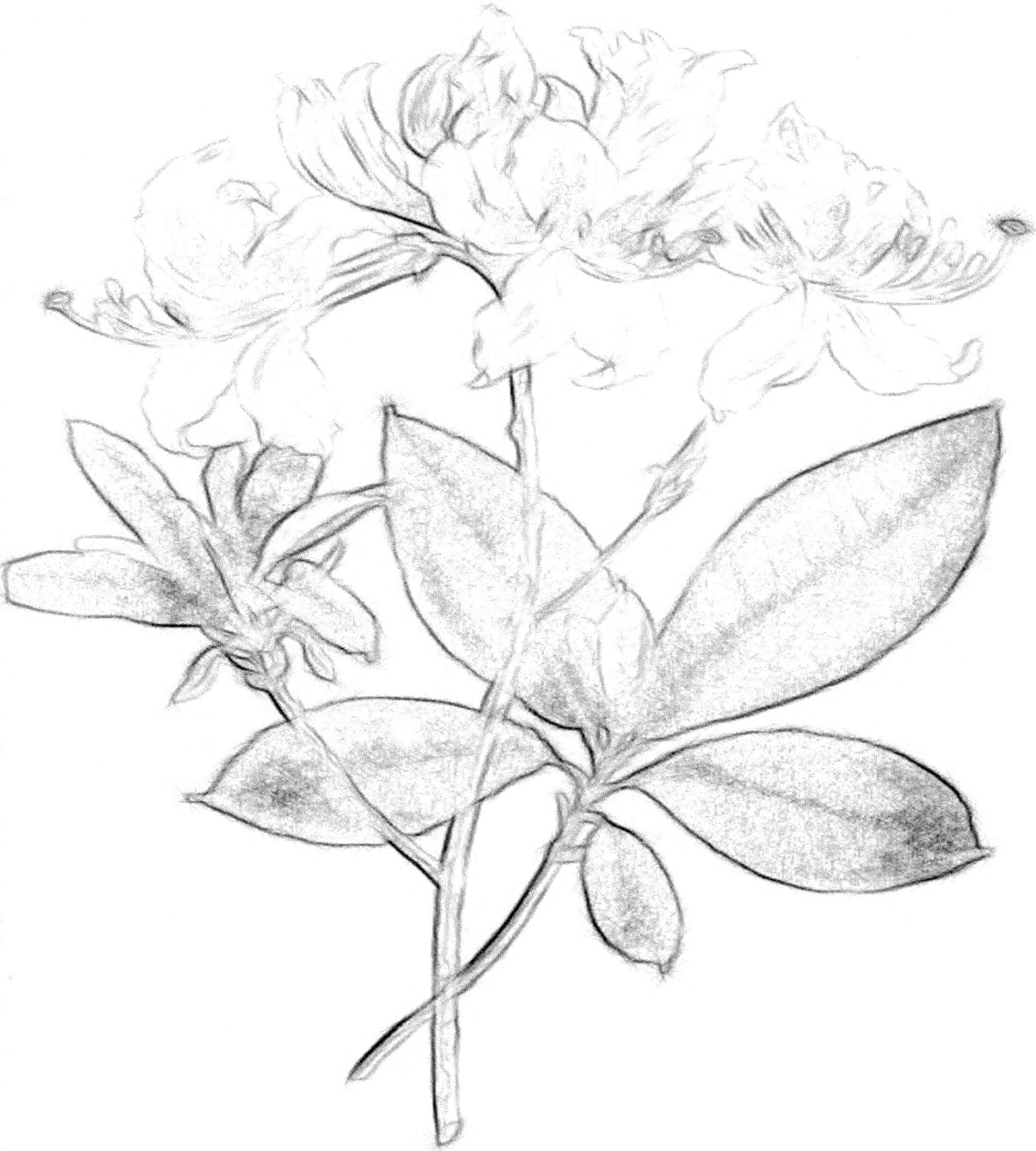

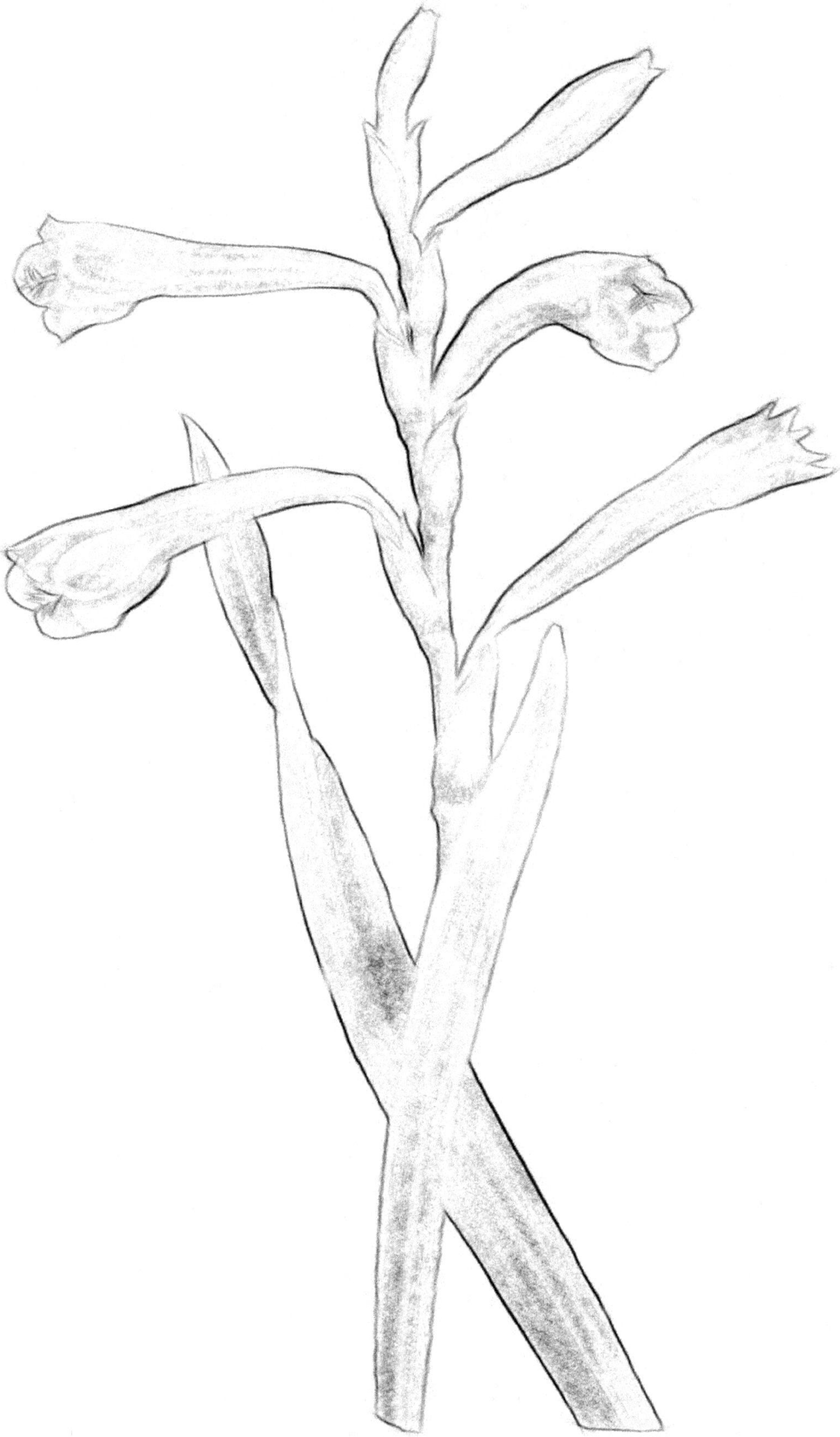

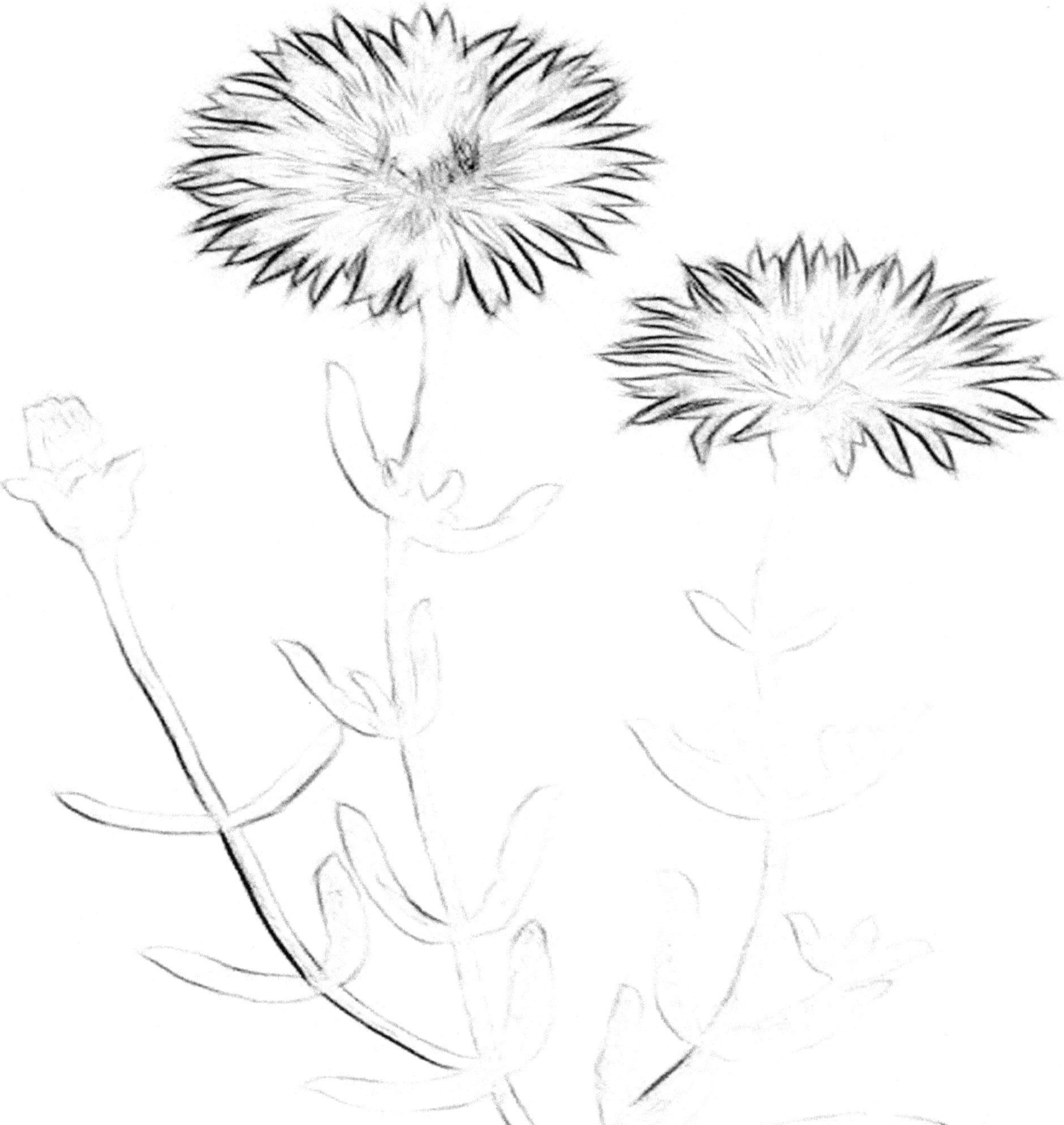

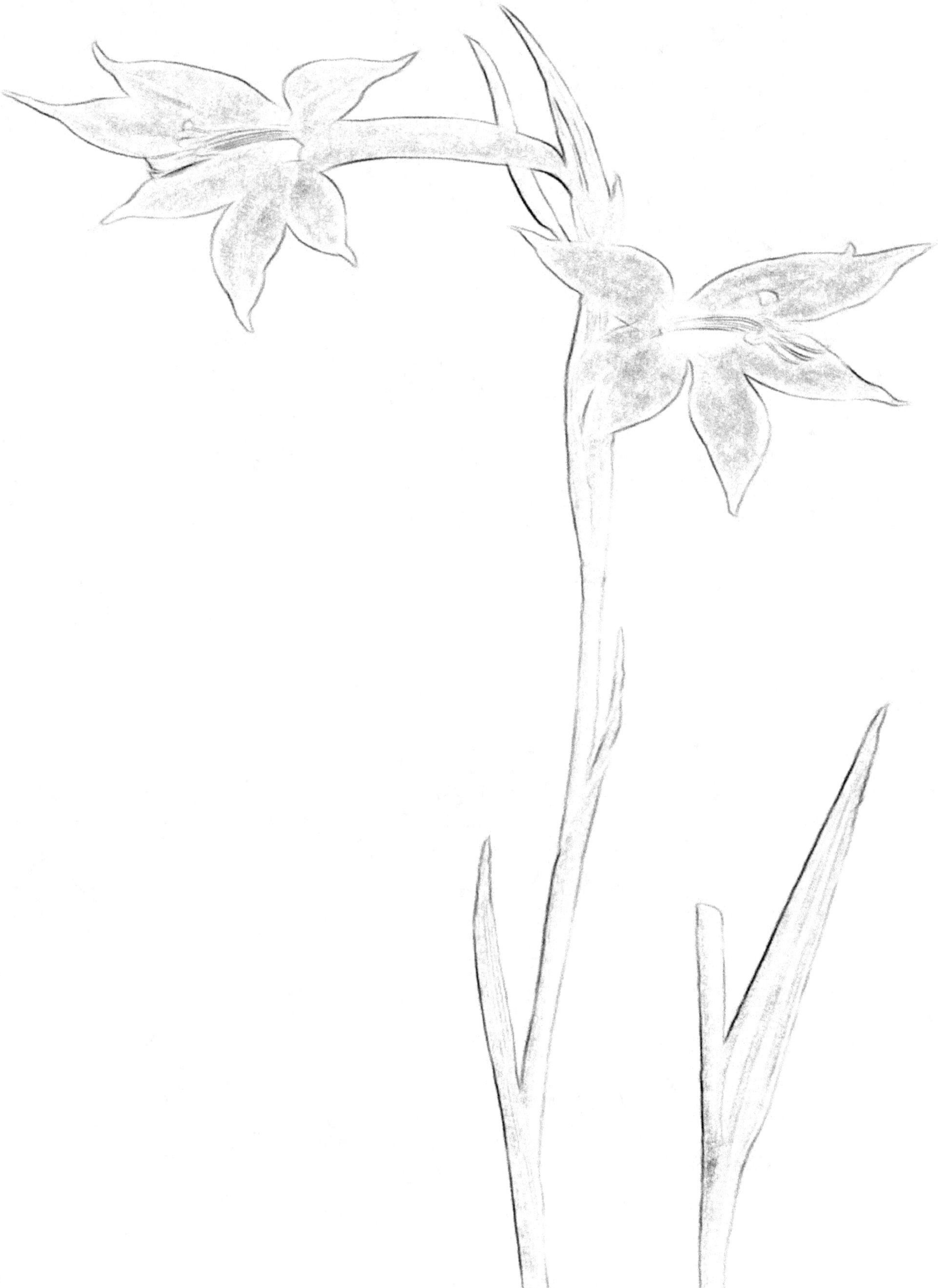

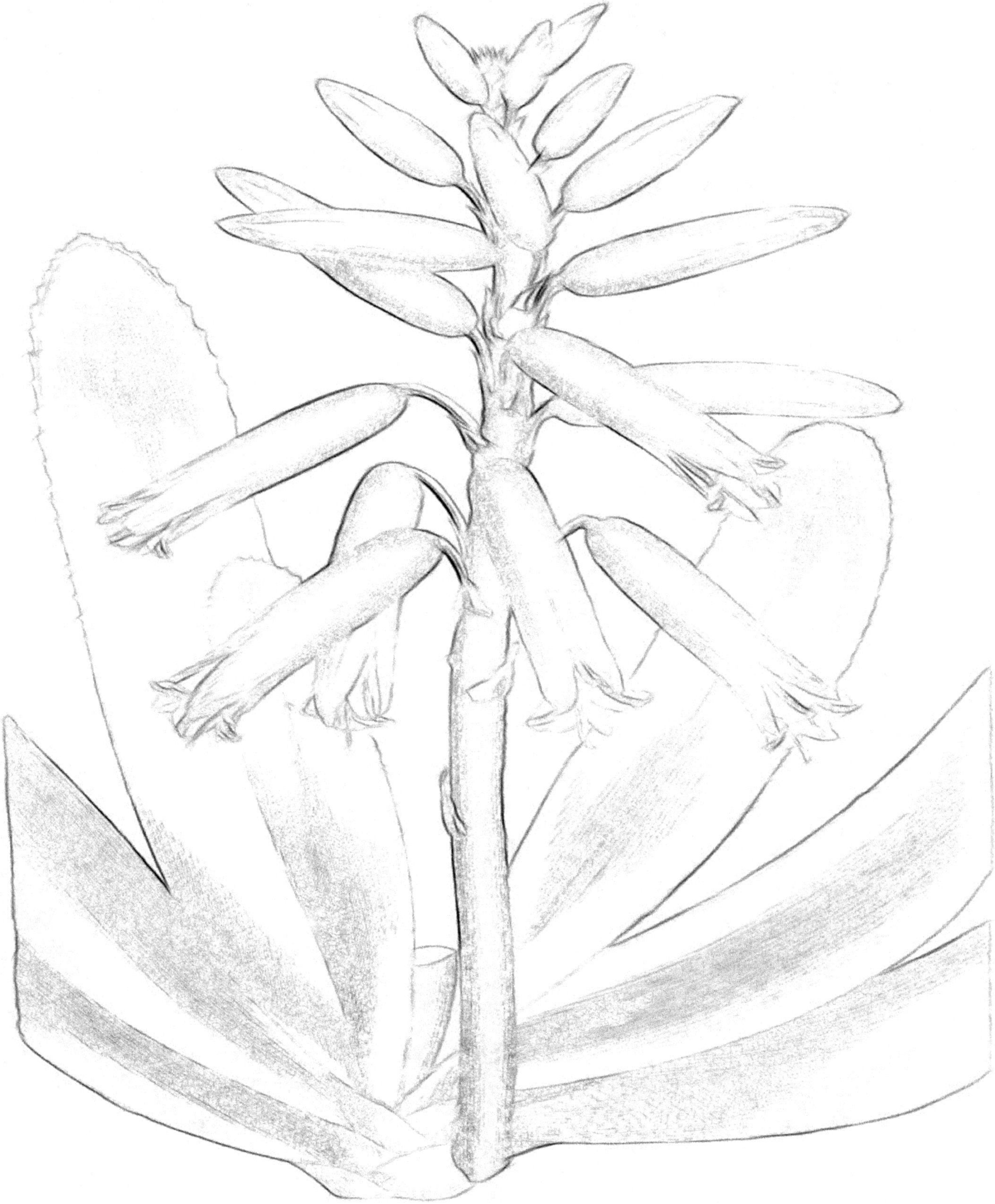

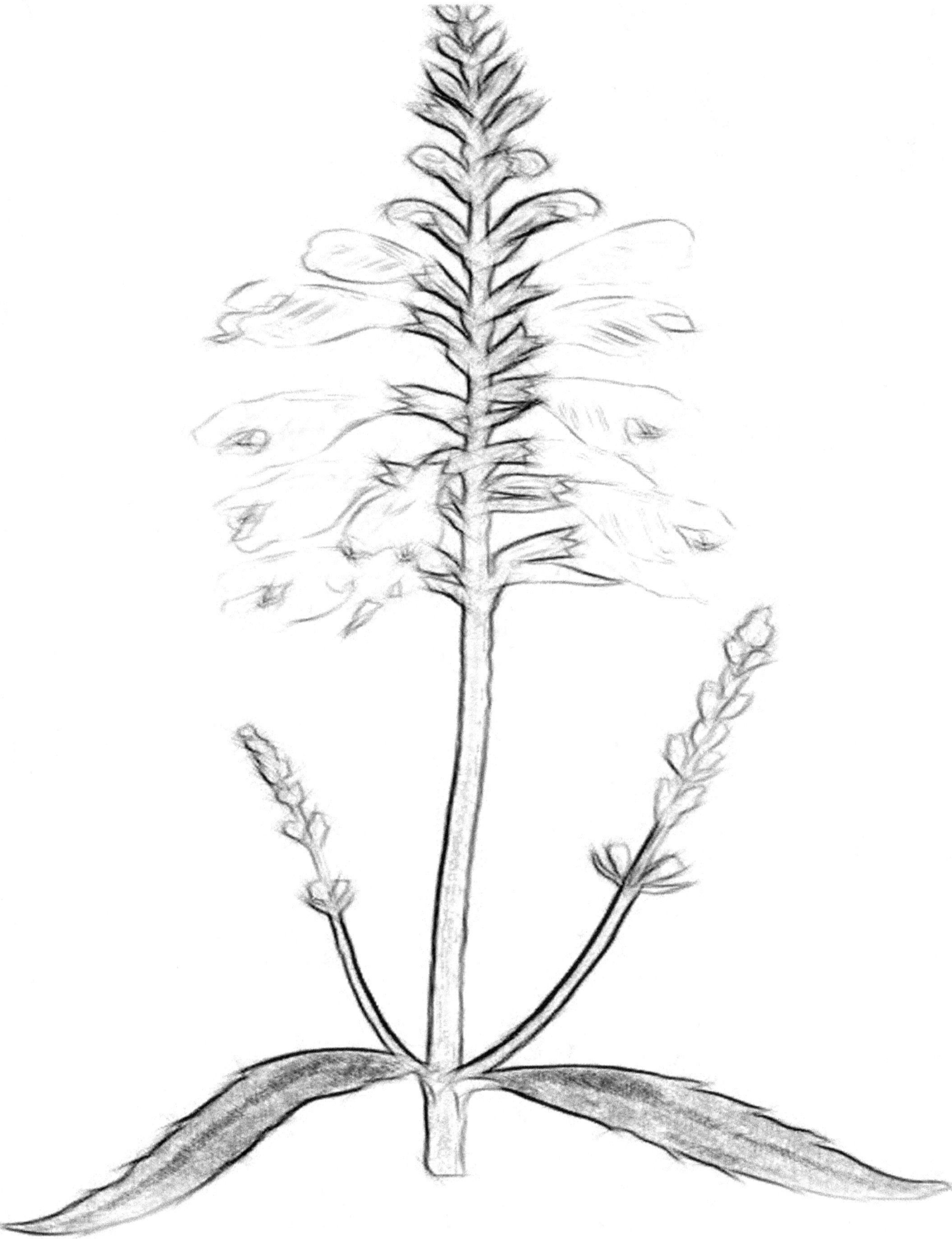

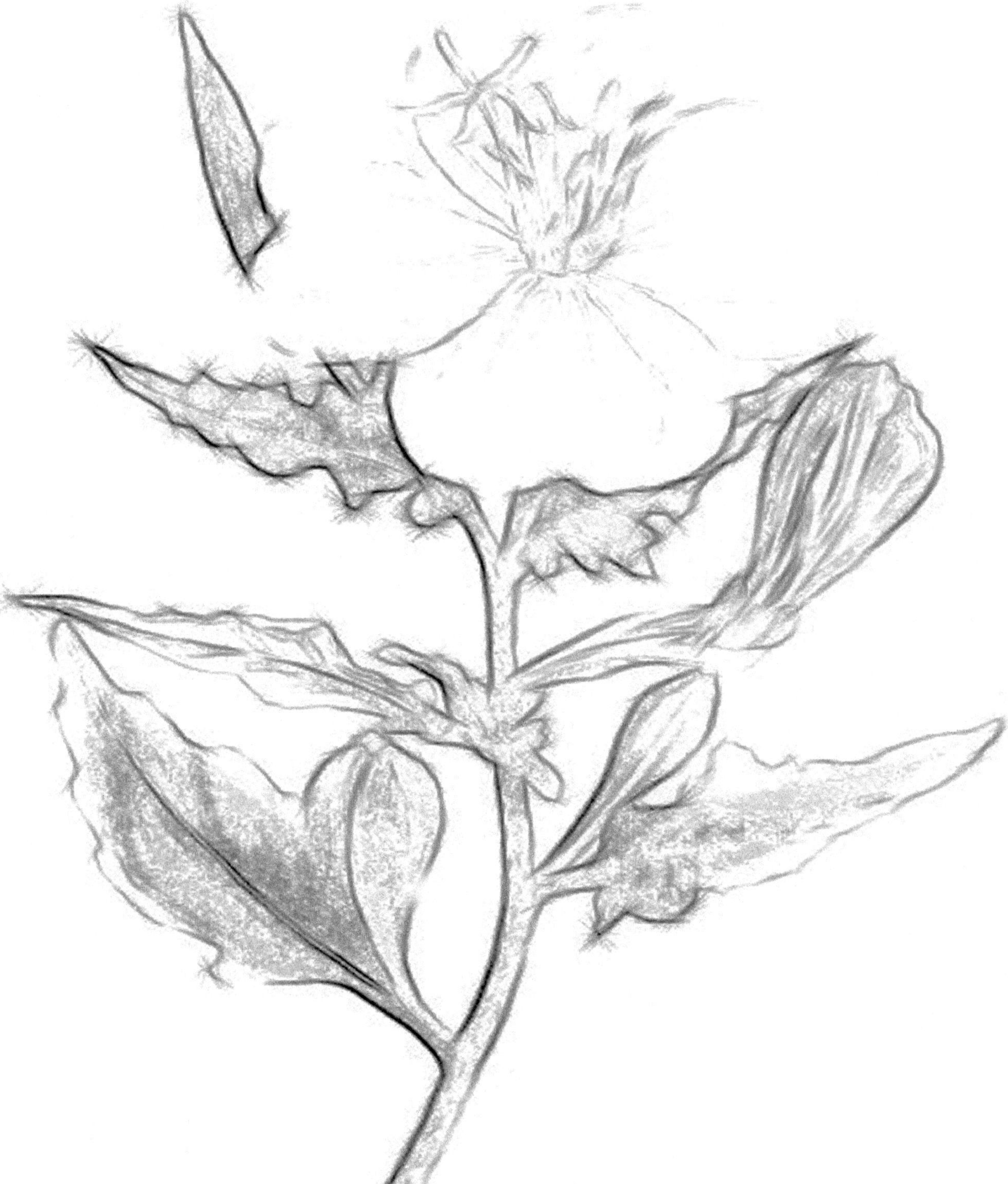

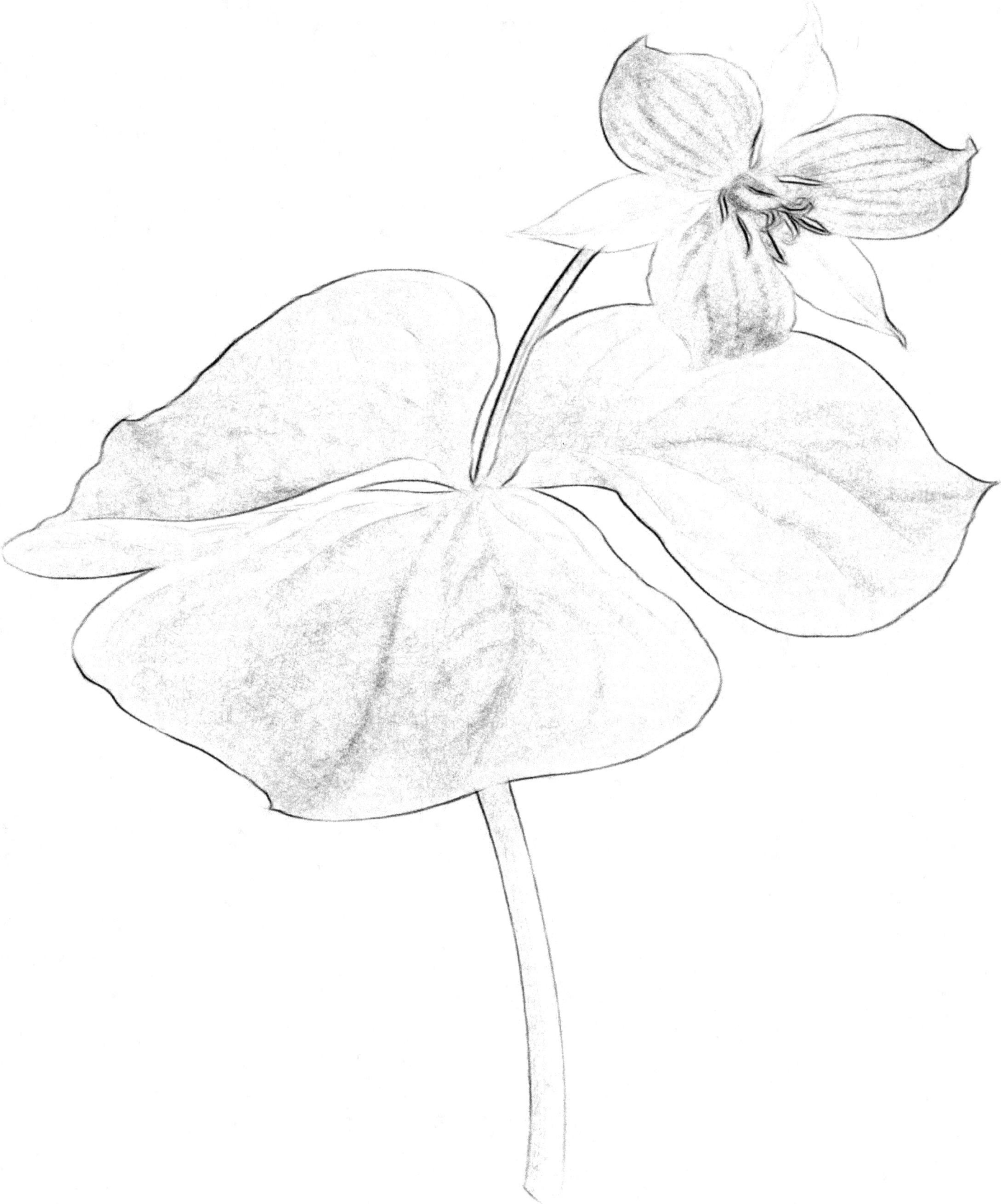

www.ingramcontent.com/pod-product-compliance
Lightning Source LLC
Chambersburg PA
CBHW081305180526
45170CB00007B/2569
9781522938712